Of Dharavi was borne, our viral present: the placenta that hangs from the hooks of global retail malls. Avikunthak's *Totem Spirit* is the prayer to the placenta to wash our innards with its globulin.

KUMAR SHAHANI

The twenties can be a time for releasing all that's raw inside, everything connected to the visceral and the carnal. These poems reflect such a moment of Avikunthak's formative *manthan*.

RUCHIR JOSHI

TOTEM SPIRIT

Ashish Avikunthak

H A W A K A L

CALCUTTA | NEW DELHI

hawakal

CALCUTTA | NEW DELHI

HAWAKAL PUBLISHERS

33/1/2 K B Sarani, Mall Road, Calcutta 80
70-B/9 Amritpuri, East of Kailash, New Delhi 65

Email info@hawakal.com
Website www.hawakal.com

First edition August, 2020

Cover art: Nanda Das
Cover design: Debleena Sen

ISBN: 978-81-946651-5-1

Price: 400 INR | USD 13.99

Preface

Does it help to label the provenance of a book of poems? If it does, then this book commenced and was finished when I lived in a city-within-a-city called Dharavi from 1996 to 1999. When Bombay was morosely mutating into Mumbai, its essence had not yet recovered from the ravages of 1992-93 riots. Dharavi was one of the flagrant epicenters of this horrific insanity. In the immensity of this apprehensive universe still smoldering, I found Dharavi a nurturing sanctuary that was compassionate and generous. But this book is not about Dharavi. Just, that its provenance is Dharavi. And the provenance of artifacts is sometimes (not always) useful in locating its affective predisposition.

I wrote poems from my late teens throughout my college life, but those were disparate reflections. It was when I moved into Dharavi, one wet monsoon day in September 1996, and I decided to write a book of verses, tentatively called Dharavi Notebook. Its narrative, structured by the location of my abode. Each of the one hundred and forty-five verses in this book was written in the ten-feet by ten-feet room I lived in. They appear chronologically in the book, with the last one penned just a few days before I quit Dharavi in November 1999.

In the last twenty years, I never made any attempts to get these published as solitary pieces in anthologies or journals because they were consciously sutured within narrative corporeality that does not have dismembered life. This book is an intricate quilt of precarious predilections, which was cautiously tucked deep inside the chest of time for more than twenty years. Now, it has been unfurled and resurrected to be aired in a new world.

Calcutta July 2020

ACKNOWLEDGMENTS

Twenty years is too late a passage of time to thank; nevertheless, here I would like to acknowledge those who graced my life during my time in Dharavi. Ganesh Shirke and his family for renting me a kholi in Dharavi during my years there. His friendship, along with the loving hospitality of his mother—the land-lady, who was exceptionally kind and affectionate. The companionship of Shrikant Agawane, and many friends who spend time with me there. Notably, the late artist Girish Dahiwale along with Riyas Komu, Justin Ponmany with whom many memorable evenings were spent writing a manifesto (still unfinished); Moloy Mukherjee, Setu, Ashim Ahluwalia, Orijit Das, Amrit Gangar, Neha Choksi and many others who passed by. Finally, Ashwini Deo for resolutely and steadfastly sharing my serendipitous and desultory life in Dharavi.

The publication of this book would not have been possible without the contagious enthusiasm of Kiriti Sengupta, who accepted this manuscript for publication with an earnestness that was humbling. There are not many publishers in India like Hawakal, who are so passionate and sincere about their commitment to the world of poetry.

I am grateful to Nanda Das for letting me use his exquisite painting and Debleena Sen for designing the elegant cover.

1

Windshield cracked, but a vision unspoiled
Honest homage to the web-original plagiarist's eventual
Congruent creations
Through which the pragmatic negotiator nonchalantly drives
He bravely seeks and navigates above men-ants crawling
Death to the dying, is not easily crushed

2

Willful exposure to the delirious heat
The slow sun seeps into my un-enameled teeth zone
Colgate made crust also withers into the intestine
Frothing above the sea level, into the mirth it perfectly pales

3

Willingness to feel a wastrel's bed sores
A tough arse gnawed by spring-cot-on-a-shovel
Bleached bed-bugs colonize across their fabled landscape
"Hark! Who goes there?"
A mantic mouth feels its own rigid arsehole
Stealthy sheathed in banana flavor
The chewing gum flavored end saturates the hostility
"But man...! Was it a fuck?"
When a perfunctory arse got screwed
On a spring-cot-on-a-shovel

4

The resilient run was suddenly aborted when
The luminous Dog flew past
A recalcitrant prisoner grasped in a grateful embrace
Could not escape
"They come of their own accord to *adee* around"
A frivolous attempt to neglect heavy bosoms
At night an oversight burst forth from his rancid stomach
Determined to escape with his convivial host
Secured in her wounded womb

5

Multifaceted interrogation manifests itself
Blanched mask obstructs veracity
In his case, the obdurate refugee answered immaculately
Thus acquitted, after his black buffalo was confiscated
Ontologically, an authentic breath cannot exist
Without nitrogen
Harbinger of truth whispers in the newsmonger's milieu
Riots did begin, without the dying, dying a death foretold
They fled from innocence into *Dharmaraja's* swarthy blotch
An imaginative conglomeration of his conveyance's feces
From living a limp subsistence
Without an enthusiastic hard-on

6

She lost her rare virginity along with him
Into the domain of adulthood, she tumbled – with Sujata
Who lost her essence along with me
In between, a cobalt cockroach was killed with
A delicate *Kolapuri*
The plastic broomstick was not used this time
Through the translucent wall, both of us could see
The desolate sun
Oblique rays skirmished past the elliptical elevation
And felt its curious warmth
"It was hot, *na*?"
In the darkness of a midday blind spot
Below the twitching of an old ceiling fan, rotating
Anti-clockwise
In mid-air, above a hollow bulls-eye
I had tragic hiccups along with her

7

A clean shaven Sikh
We saw him prancing through crimson trees in a bland
Blockbuster
Wooing a *Tara* and her conspicuous assets
Featuring instead of an authentic Man
They hurriedly smooch only for the tattered silver screen
Wasting initiatives of real-life
In reel-life, he imitates the Gods of Bollywood
Once in a while, the scheming *Sardar* drinks
Lassi churned in traditional Washing Machines

8

Ghost stories shared by grandmother resting in
Perpetual Peace
Scares the nylon umbrellas to open before touchdown
The albatross amongst them sinks to the soft bottom
And saves the dead guy, of a poet's fragmentary figments
Counting copper coins in hidden Piggy banks
Somber children in nightclothes sleep together at dawn
Tired of waiting for the presumptuous grandma
To wake up from a deep slumber
And recite tender lullaby of blue baseball caps
Repeating what they learnt from capricious coffin makers
Of middle America

9

A wax door locked
Overweight men were barking orders
To dogs in golden chains, behind it
Hostility acute in banana peel season
A *Gita* was given free to landlords along with *Nirodh*
Like toothbrushes, free with an onion
In air-conditioned Supermarkets
Independence was granted, but *Gita* continued to stay

10

Wet my room
From the corner you begin and, it will spread
Slowly into my freckled world
Your reticent shivers torment my loop-holed sentiments
As I see you see at an end
Exhausted, while children are still playing with
Solid Symmetries
Heaven poured when we made the seesaw for them
It was Lord's gift anyway
Thanks to Him, the community piss-pot did not overflow
Today

11

Sophisticated snag discovered
In the disgruntled lock of the black-box
Corrupted curator of the house
Could have got his job jacked up
If my mama had not nominated her Queen
While deposing the other. She check-mated
Dhanagare's choice
On the chessboard, of a soliciting firm's law-school intern
The black was melting and thus the white showed up
In the game of lock and key, one had to loose
Or probably both
Resigned, the gray was cornered by both colors
And the box was not found after the car-crash

12

From the point of bold gravity
An impressive compromise lay lax
Two cocks met petulantly; sad
Dilated balls assumed nicknames; lost
Sobriety dawned on copious intentions
Tautologically, it meant a hard-on without a jerk
A ponderous delight for those
Who do not want to read any further

13

Pink cheeks, in crowded shadows, sell convoluted
Guidebooks
Cognition maps direct hustlers through unarmed sides
From the slum city they maneuver crippled pawns
Feigning surreptitious deals. Lawmakers are brought
Paid in counterfeit with colloquial overshoots
Sleepless hawkers perform gladly with succulent tongues
Every weekend, when irked wives are together, underground
Mangalsutras are false symbols of marital status
Whereas *kumkums* are used to color red bottoms, more red
Fondling each other's burgeoning assets
The husbands are the divine devils
The softer dames do not disappear all at once
At the fleeting backdrop of a flaky doubt
The lawbreaker and the lawmaker redraft
A fallen Constitution

14

The dead man slept; mud-deep; knee-deep
Incense smoke stroked the sullen air
In the big conglomeration's medical school
First year students fainted during Anatomy Practical

15

Through a horizon tonsured; privately
Without cynical ceremony
Harmony rustic, presumed in a staggering decorum
One rupee fine levied for not talking in English
We hush up as the Father trots past, nodding in Malayalam
Verbal abuse, often un-conceitedly unabashed
A jest provokes demure pride to snub me
Swapping technique well-versed in pilfering a fallacious fraud
While a quirk surfaces in a craze for cultish banquets
An evening vertigo pierces the spectral hatch
The final concussion looming in the meandering thought
The estranged alliance lapses into a tattooed laugh
A free fall through the coterie of select gender-less-ness

16

Pellucid clarity transmitted from dumb tube lights
Their frosted bleach smudges a neutral tint
Legs of a little girl walk past like a fleeced prodigal
An amputated hand, bewildered; conscious of its own vivacity
Cannot grope through a daughter's convulsion
Aluminum fly-swatter fiercely clutched
It snaps the twang rabidly
A masked mosquito camouflaged on the mole of her left thigh
Escapes to the constellation of eleemosynary stars

17

A Head closely guarded by baroque butterflies in dogfights
Mating with air bubbles autographed by a bellicose boxer
In love with endorsements, substantiated at every lost bout
A mushroom-cut or a blunt-cut is the secret protected
By flighted masses of metamorphosed genius
Two teeth also jut out for the Rabbit *Bhayia* to be complete
Split ends lead to two beginnings at the end
One oiled and the other sun burnt at night
From within – a command to commence attention, is profound
In case of capricious origin
Diligent dogs are divorced from quixotic wars
She at the dinner walked out of my life with rose water
Just-in-case

18

Ever met an unresponsive woman under the bed?
A blunt paunch fixated on intent; Query
Cloth-less on a *Hussaini Chaddar*
She is a wry witness discovered
Feet sniffed
And the flapping rubber *chappals* assaults a nostril
When kissed they shrug away from redolent overtures
Her thin gait clogs a soft aperture; crossing a barren boundary
Wriggling under the blanket
The whimsical wall is tenderly touched
Bricks clutch the beauty – thickness is measured
Inch-by-inch
To demean the crouched corner with frozen assertions
What do you mean by responsive alignment?

19

Myriad are the belief systems of a visiting cowherd
On a one-wheel bicycle, he issues promulgation; Knighted
The apocalyptic city in eternal state of mirth
And, bloodless feuds; starved
Its egregious insignia installed behind *Krsna's* clumsy throne
His virtual attempt
To pervade the solidity of content, continues beyond
Constructed in a monochromatic cartoon strip with
Peanut playing piano
The composition tumbles sonorously
And, the audience snores without doubt

20

"Ajit!"
The call pitted against myriad dream cells
Confronted in the freckled corner of my own convoluted blur
Separating sheep intertwined; fantasies bleat in cleavages
The trajectory penetrates the mosquito net into the shout
"Ajit!"
Was she not calling for you?
Or it is always for me?
"Ajit!"

21

Forbidden Happy Hunting Ground; aghast
The run along the waterhole crucified to a single lucent drop
Warm blood flowing in spurts; the wound, fatal
On a sunmica school desk mesmerized by Jim Corbett
Not alone, but with a faithful hunting tiger's nail
Wobbling on the hairy breast, a *mangalsutra*
Espoused to the
Rummaging of Dead Man Eater; left
Nuptials in a tale of a philanthropist's telling
In slow motion they dig deeper, where veins pulsate
The claws of a virtuous wife, pending an astonished divorce
A deceitful drum bellies in the divine dark
A happy, Happy Hunting Ground warmly welcomes him

22

Chastity protected; a man over the uncovered
Cluttered with possibilities
As the walk on the succulent toes begins
An angelic quilt too small to cover each other's desuetude
We stumble on a hard rock and the world sees her naked soul
An hourglass shattered but time-keeping continues
But she could not cover herself up again; ever
In the portrait of the nude, colors were permanent
I walked over the earth, feeling the flocculent scabs
On her adamantine back

23

Following footprints around a bronze casket, overturned
The impetuous energy-swing, shows me her anguished face
You were she, my mother in triplicate
Three times you gave birth to me
But I was not born. Even once

24

Frisking Tetra-pods – resting after a trajectory cut short
Here, preventing the collapse of an effortless city-drive
Vindicating the thought of zooming *Marutis*
Retreat inside, when crabs crawl over-leaf, mutely
Wait at the total crack of the dawn
As the millennium is delivered forth
It fortuitously slides into the pale sea
Now the crabs preserve the homogeneity of
A roadside's incongruity

25

Fired with reverence and love, a mass-housing complex
Commits suicide, unsuccessfully
Fiends from the Goose-trap land come to pay homage, also
Here dusty Gods with their vast retinue, reluctantly reside
Tied to the umbilical cord of their energy-consorts
Everyone plays Ludo and Chess in a heavenly sense
Xeroxing each strategy for display
At the Co-Op Society's notice-board
Communal, an exercise to emphasize one man-ship
With polytheistic paganism
Pre-puberty wives of their diligent devotee do not grow old
In the center of their drained gadgets, blood is not passed
Remember, even then
Lonely Gods commit incest with flavored condoms

26

Radio jingles dipped in water bottles – going to School
Dragging frugal breakfast in an aluminum tiffin box
Rubber stitched; temporarily
An eight-minute walk, faster than a drawling tramcar
Salvaging a languor in a knight's move
On a chessboard, school and home
Share a confronting destiny
A doting mother's status symbol; punished for
Taking a leak, without praying to a perpetually pregnant Mary
Stooping on the second floor's corner
Bearing God's infinite burden
Fun is duplicated, in triplicate
Favorite football field is measured by a cigarette butt; twice
Dear Father, after-school roams in his wife's white nightie
It was a ghost story seen during Mr. *Srivastava's* Hindi period

27

Look at the public fuming at the demented site
Walking on a streetcar named – Stammering Tango
Policed by Home Guards suckling surrogate rubber nipples
Managing a free flow of devotees to witness a miracle; doomed
On the last day of the world
A swollen tart shows her brilliant arse to Buddha "hooded"
Delivering a Sermon from Vatican on the Channel
Felicitating Favorite Fellowmen under Funky Foliage
Disallowed to dig Nose in Public, instead
He gently digs Public in Nose
"Those who have attained Nirvana can stand in the queue
Even without an appointment letter"

28

The archaic river descends into the ascent of luring abyss
Of her blurred navel
As the ancestors defined the mesmerizing myth
Quit flowing a Vermin on the Mount
Redeeming Khaki sacrificed on swirling scaffolding
The transitory God of blind reality
Seeking contours of the bounce
"Stuff it with sardines"
He launches a dystopic discourse, into an ethereal space
"Nine, eight, seven, six, five, four, three two, one, zero"
The baleful backfire loses a proxy war
A poker faced disciple collects Monopoly money
Stares cold bloodedly
Into eyes, who secretly defecate
On the sandy banks, at midnight
Jupiter tonight has loaned us the third moon
Encroachment legitimized
Knowledge was at the corner, but the river only got dammed

29

Corrugated asbestos sheets defiant
When Gods go to Dogs, they petulantly pray
To Future Flies and Sumica Table-Tops
Tending families in mass-housing complexes
Through the water tap, the television images flow, haltingly
They gingerly walk around in circumambulatory circles
And tend to fail
In their endeavors to save the Holy skin from rusting

30

Animal forest stands in the low valley
Of anonymous stool-pigeons
Sacred to men who marry each temperamental tree
Worship her and
Ejaculate on her augmented vulva
Till she gives birth to our sad-kind in the middle of nowhere

31

Without the Mother, in the Harem of the lonely Lord
Children are born to women but not to his whimsical Wife
Was it I, then, which was born?
The bloody cycle was feigned to trick his coveted finger
The rubber was found unused
Or was I, a son of a bitch?
Resulted after the pin-holed condom gave in?
And without consent, I surged forward; surreptitiously

32

They scream around the ochre circle and, I cannot sleep
Black sheep stubbornly withhold their fresh wool
They are carefully herded; and make fertile, fields of food
Droppings are revered and *Bhajans* are rendered soullessly
Shree Krsna has finally returned, to be lazy at home

33

A steel chopper is swished in the service of another Mother
Blood thirsty; red in color
Tongue of gold
Surrounded by soiled dhotis and crisp currency notes
Held between stained teeth; strangled by deformed teeth
Her slit wide open, vermilion smeared with maternal love
For the fingers of my mother
Only can slide to touch the corrugated wall
Hung on the opaque facade, not fallen to be picked up
Unformed at the edge, extremities are deformed
The stainless steel does not miss its mark
At the center, gravity lets the fallen to still fall further deep

34

Flying at the furthest corner of the Universe of Agents
Disturbing Peace of Mind of a Time-out watch
A Tornado and wooden clots come up simultaneously
Tragic comic combination does not fail at the Box-office
Wooden clots are left out and laughed at
To pacify the Tornado with snarling snails

35

Bucolic barber in the Comb Shop
Voices of defeat lament the destruction of a jagged soul
The libidinous nun was raped to make *Lucia* cry
She was the suggestive Soothsayer of spasmodic quirk
Paranoid about the hair fall
He surfaced at the egg-yolk shop, also
She whispered through the netted screen
With her restive breasts
And, her innocent navel, heavy with ambush
The *Stalker* with plaintive eyes
Was the one, the placid creator was fond of
A vanishing vision in the ominous web
The Shaman of the Earth and Night is finally inter-net-ed

36

A weird home, on the ground floor, under the *Khaitan* fan
Swinging with no notion of motion; solemnly
Late for a dinner, we forgivingly slept below
The oscillating circle
Khadi mosquito net
Is the non-violent defense, in the homecoming story
Covered with her grandfather's crocheted shawl
And sullen sheets hidden from a dry-cleaner's scintillating gaze
Pasted permanently with *Fevicol* in God's frame

37

Admonished, in the winter of Dead Man and Yellow Sugar
Tripped over the passing train track and he had to forever wait
For the first time, four locals zoomed one after another
Above a starless night, below a loitering God
Anticipating a thrust from a reminiscent peerage
He saw himself bungling a misdirected flat fall
Ill-contrived conception acquires a ready audience
On the blood stained train tracks, somberly fell silver coins
The dead man crawled with a disgruntled grin

38

Between the water bay and a cowardly mongrel
A turgid day passes tugging the drudgery of the night along
Surprisingly, the species of this kind are allowed
Without tin number-plates
Sheepish, the dawn and the twilight sinks noiselessly
During High Tide
Various bawdy songs are soullessly manifested
Sung in unison by Night Walkers of the naked Beach
A visage of few-mouthed Dragon
Blooms in a titanium flower-pot
The flame flickers and a dreamscape is brilliantly burnt
Hoping for the Shopping Train of Thugs to halt it

39

The assassin shot the absconding God and fled, homewards
In the borrowed *Dictator Studebaker*, puffing on an empty road
The Radiator gave away and the police caught him
The killer was named, stamped, still-used, like always
Never won an award at Vintage Car Rally
Statesman was not his favorite newspaper
It was *Nathuram's*
Getaway vehicle; not at the scene of the crime
Hidden behind a prison-wall forever, condemned
Till they graduate to cycles rickshaws
Hand rickshaws
And, auto rickshaws
To walk away from the same scene of the crime

40

Resurgence in the children's park. A flat football bounced
On a cricket pitch; crater formed and the *durban* saw it
Ran inwards. *Lathi*-charged with sticks of a hockey match lost
He umpired. Scatterbrains
We are all fifteen. Fifteen *Holies* we shot
The Canon of the Water Balloons
Could not catch us; famished he stopped, tired
Another football bounced on a cricket pitch
Craters were naturally born on this part of the black moon

41

In the pigeon-hole of dead darkness
Contempt of lurid shade, committed
Judicial court, conscientious
Prudently procrastinated a judgment
Death by hanging till dead, announced latter
Baseball cap lowered
And, a trot towards Beginning begin, slowly

42

The first fight ensues; the fist-fight in the obscure alley
Through the collar-holding action, variety is expounded
It is a piratical raid. Two men protect a garrison fort
Gizmos are resorted to. Yesterday was contemporary
Today is antiquity
Ideal of a forsaken appendage, left in the municipal morgue
To protect wildlife. To save a selfish self

43

Tarnished myth commits to euphony
Charlatans chant in the *garbha-griha.* Temple of Lords
Maligned and in dis-usage; on Eternity Bed
Vibrations plod on the hiccups of a pot-holed legend road
"Hero ducks the arrow shot. Villain dies a hero's death"
Inhabitants of Clutter Heaven, not yet exalted
In the realm of the flagitious God
Who foresaw the acquisition drive, fail
He announced pack-up before the seventh day
Mutual benevolence in Manhood acquires a benefit of doubt

44

Between an unborn anticipation and a new-born birth
Fecund origin is frequently fertilized
And ceaseless death is prevented; un-supposed birth
Cries to announce its faithful war
Bursts forth a receptacle. Chewing tobacco
Venerable earth soaked to a divine depth
Within a peaceful co-existence, verbosity in discord
Is rendered redundant, thoughtlessly
Formless shadows are not, what were wanted
But, it is a defined end in itself

45

Acquiescence. Performance repudiating natural enemies
Pawn committed to a sacrifice. Queen
Hunger of a flamboyant river, satisfied

46

Un-fulfilled diet on a walk. A blind alley sidelined
The night un-slept by the world
Ostensibly, a *Ramzan* praising its Zion
Picking, Hoof in the Mouth disease at random
Immaculate digestive delinquency – culpable
Lapses in the Fasting. Rituals, unworthy of it are banned
Present in obdurate religion. Guarded zealously by zealots
Conservatives sneak into the room, shyly
In a *Zenana Khanna*; stoned. A queue
Is formed. Impotent men wait for their turn to see

47

Manicured feet, prepare for a Wedding Circuit
Nail polish not-spread. Mehndi well-spread
Seven times, she circumambulated the fire hearth's emptiness
Poised nervously on quaintly fashioned red stilettos
Quivering under her own sex; she suddenly slumps
Into the cascade of Cactus Flower Garden
Consecrated use inspires the grace to surreptitiously seep in
The pores. The pious is blessed. The husband is followed
With hesitation

48

The Saturday Night Fever or the Monday Morning Blues
Two days separated by a Sun-Day
The day when the Wall goes into hiding
New Broom in action, solicits praises
Fuss is clinched to officiate a soft snap of a nap
Search for hoary whores
Gives way to a wife's delightful delicacy
Wine, transformed in a Bottle-to-Bottle kiss
Sneaks without murmur. Spurs a moment of truth
Stirs into the somber niches of the sunny Day

49

Coolly coiled at the unraveled corner of the coveted Circle
Helpless Heroine of a frolicsome spiral, whirls, sinking
Deep within a Twist; an arid movie begins
Flexing and re-flexing in the crux of the confusion
The end is shown twice, flea-bitten by a florid vision

50

"Phonetic gyration, smothers an eloquence"
One to thirteen – a song negates the rest of the numerals
Numbers hanging on a fissured tongue
Acknowledged masterpiece; a ruckus in a coquette-corner
Vocalized. Intonation connected to an imperious master

51

Sleep, felicitated in a car-back at Jaws
She pinches my arse and walks away with a hole
I wanted to enter and, see her at work
Through the peephole, customers can't see
While we placidly play
Games at war
Feeble children hit mercury marbles to enter me
Choked, I survive; her fingers in my rapacious mouth

52

Hue of delicate transparency; tainted in its hallucinating haze
It slips gazes of sleep in dreams; mouth gaping
And vividly conscious of its own vivaciousness
Timid amethyst, found in your cheeks bones
Shape an impassive face
Felt rime before the melt down near her brittle face
Flawless azure separates its hallowed iridescences
All over. Clear sighted, Color Purple is the one
Looking at the world of subterranean streets
"Selling fashion with one hand, one leg, one soul, one eye"

53

Freeborn in frenzy; born from the inscrutable womb
Of a Mother. My man of many colors is a blotch
Fumbles his limp self to a surprise without endeavors
Distinguished evil does not slip into his underwear, unattended
He separates the celibate and enters the off-white petticoat
To hide Scratching-Balls meant for Foot-Balls
His own nickel zip-fastener about to give way
Too tight to curb the fragile bulge
Hides behind a *Burkha* shedding its blackness; or in it
Sujata remarks: "The brain spattered on the road
Is also black"

54

The Who
Was looking for babes in the bath water?
Obeisance, he paid to no one in it; only empty water
The drizzle drained the forest fire into, in it
Life survived and babies were born once again
Then, Who was it, who saw himself in It?

55

Smoothen niche of a Power to be, in basalt – menstruating
Carved by stoic men touching their Mother's sullen surface
Deliberately, devoting their Sin, to an empty edifice
A hardened stump, dexterous – moves to the right
Left-handed followers, sure-footed, rhythmically flow inside
Suffered, she unmasks her spectacular charade
Of delicious intricacies
In the floral labyrinth
Clawed by radiant nymphs gossiping irreverence
She dotingly guides
Only devoted men through her venereal orifice
An impeccable vulva is formed at the birthplace
Of the eighty-one-petalled Lotus

56

At the assertive embarkation, before the First Move
Was initiated
An inevitable conclusion was unanimously sought
Betrothed flourishing was courteously seized
And tragically deprived
"When everyone was female; we became male"

57

On the dry Waterfront
An incandescent garden does not extinguish
Saved, by the Brave New Generation
Endowed with suspicious warts
Cracks. In the month of May, the mayflower blooms
Voluptuously
Made in twenty-seventh Heaven
They are covertly sold on scorched Earth
Packed in cellophane and red ribbons leftover
For Birthday mornings. They reach home exhausted
Breathless
Celebrated by one Pure Man in Love
A multi-colored guy with pants down, at-ease, Nowhere
But at-tension, Here. In my blemished house

58

Man, manning a manhole – open
Prevents malfunctioning men
From falling with their splendid Taxies
Blindfolded driver manages to get into the
Limca Book of Records
Tipsy with lime juice he falls with his watchful Taxi
Hole on the wretched road is wide, now
On a flooded monsoon morning – dark, heavy and sad
Hardworking men fall without their faithful Taxies
But with themselves

59

Molestation with knotted hands in the hiding and, a burnt kiss
In a white night, looking for sullen whores
No one complete is ever found
Hide and Seek game turned suggestively sour
Half-male-half-female
Showed up. Nothing incomplete, but without etcetera
Split-sex appointed with divine grace and mercy in Hair
Congenial entity immaculately seduced by
Magical material in Spirit
The Speedwell hits for the Loo to loosen his timid gestures
Here. There is nothing except myself
He the king of the All-Here-People
From that time onwards
Is the frail God not able to stir his singularity?

60

An estranged quest, takes an agonizing escape route
The serene night-runner, runs away from an unknown garb
Unable to fear, he can't even face it
Let alone, confront it during the end of the time
Resuscitated by the Temple-of-the-Toe-of-the-Right-Foot
During the circle of worship, when all becomes radiantly red
At the kernel of a tranquil city
Inherited from the emblem of regeneration
He brings *chappatis* to instigate a sincere rebellion
After half a century of precarious independence
Multiple leakages
Inundates the sagacious Valley

61

Conquest in the fallacy mirror-scape of crooked reflection
To See
From side-to-side, cracks appearing. Reflection corrupts It
The matter rendering its curious apathy; a moral play
Synoptic in device, muse and consummate skill
Irony is cajoled to give Judas a kiss-on-his-arse
Evading in false color, an undercover Fish Story
Retreats from an aggression penetrating hard water
Reflecting a magnification of boneless fish
Whereas the unforgettable Seen is not seen
It only frantically pierces into the mirror image of It

62

Counting streets; contemplating on streets; murder on the street
Lessons by-hearted from studying the hierarchy of the street
In the city center, they all meet and collate to exchange
When the organic city was formed, planning was cogitated
To thwart the urban night to be twice born
Fallible intimacy can be seduced into verbosity of comradeship
In the family circle, neighborhood took to aloofness
A voluntary exile to move away from acquaintances
The coterie of Loved-ones
Looked-ones
Lasting-ones
Loose-ones
Therefore, to plan an urban security is a misnomer
The impulse to discover the right kind of nomenclature
Is natural by placing streets and streets and streets
In proximity, to convenience all sections of the square

63

The flat city, re-oriented
A product of the speculated landmass
Kissing the sky or the sky is the limit, which is true?
But, *Dronagiri* also bent down into its earthiness
Dronacharya dug pond here, pond there, pond everywhere
Skilled with a different kind of a memory
And looking through the eye-of-a-fish or a fish-eye-lens
The twin across the city was a function of containment
The vitality of the city was a point missed; incidentally
In it nothing had meaning, only utility value
Build on the corridor of demand, notwithstanding unevenness
Desecrating the village iconography
The city was born with a bad karma
To decongest the elder twin, leaking and bursting from within
At the sides and around uneven corners
It was the dormitory of the Greater City
Where no one ever slept

64

What was it, that we saw? Sujata, you and me?
In the cry-baby zone, of a kindergarten fashion
You preferred metrical motifs
With archetypes alive and throbbing
In the style of mammoths, elks, bison and tempestuous waves
With color-coded ends and threatening Turkish scimitars
Hacking, at the finish of the city-riots, the stalks in shade
They were detached from the Flowers of the Holy Well
School children gather here and laugh
When memories troop in
And, Sujata, you did not go for the march-past
In This, is what, why do you question?

65

Lull between harsh showers of a monsoon's giving, is natural
Jubilation astound even Him of the Pulled One
His cute car, pushed and pulled by his own defiant kids
Wobbles
Grievous colors pour slowly. Is washable in detergent
Chanting mundane mantras with straw-piped *Coca-Cola* cans
Propagating vegetarian-goodness
To the sea of printed umbrellas
It is an adulterous generation, He does not care about
Slick Bhakti-Yoga with stilted American accent
The Supreme unstable or the Stumped mascot is handicapped
Abandons his overeating cousin in a crowded street
Falls madly in love
With his fecund female devotees, faithful to him
Radha to Him; He is *Krsna* to them

66

Vagabond messages, were you not hiding?
My love letters in your burnt leather purse
Reading in leisure, Sujata would toss them back one-by-one
So many Sujatas; so many letters; so many of love
Stacked neatly
I read them to a new Sujata, every time

67

Cotton mosquito net was a shroud of perforated admissions
To prevent malignant malaria. In it she gazed hopelessly
With my brother, I slept at the Sujata-corner
Crawling lizards in housetop scared her; eyes sordid
Lubricated with *Odomos*, love was interrupted
In the intimate stowaway of things, prevention was often foiled
The whispering evidence of play was heard
On the other side of the innocent word
Struck with malaria, weeks were lost in diligent delirium
Of love songs, hate and an added pregnancy

68

Clothed as an unfettered man, at cardinal points, a soft slave
The father of a God-sent-information-freak-shot
Son of an admonished sage in sordid fashion
The newspaper, he reads; but ignores the crooked crossword
At the nightly hour the prodigal son solves it
And forgets to see a mild nightmare in slow slumber

69

The memories of an affectionate tree are buoyant at the center
Ever growing rings of the bark do not wither
In them are concealed Pressure, Load and Burden
Scale deepens their ceremonial assertion, to gravitate its yoke
To associate its cumbersome body with firmament's host
Poised to plunge into the sanctity of doubt
A remembrance discovered when a venture succeeded
An echo sounded; shivers runs through earth to sky
Huddled up at the Sujata-Climb
It recognized her naked footprints on the forlorn leaves
Love was a fragment at the time of His Colorful Stamina

70

Moment to moment, in the unpropitious time
The call to cook in the frying pan is unheeded
Dire visit of a Cockerel ruins the event of stalking
The married woman knocks its head, in one stroke
Overwhelmed with a durable wrath, it hits the floor
An ill-omen seized by its neck
The male effigy's mouth cannot eat
Now, it does not even open

71

That very day
On the Ides of May, hot, when summer is still swelling
Tar emerges to form a miraculous mirage on the Road
Sticks a footprint in itself; the pressure plate gives away
Photograph of a man-pug-mark falls through a manhole
The hole
In black-water the frozen first step is consequently cooled
The thousand feet journey was now an abrupt statement
Adroit legwork under the crowded city stopped
Above it, the car rolled and overtook its sorry space

72

Silver shells in aquarium, that which goes round
Not in circle but around, a world away
Without straight lines
In it, with sellers of bra-straps – elastic and cotton
To up-keep acacia blossoms from falling down
Balancing between languishing cleavages, *mangalsutra* of dawn
Shell motif of bliss is why the two are together
And the cup catches the circle with straight-lines

73

The trouble in the fish-pot world, is its succulent stink
Every corner had the fish-eater smacking and belching
Then also, the Mahatma on currency notes
Meditates on the fish
Government was keen to display solidarity
To the estranged Father of the Nation
Without a mother; only fish
The Hero knew well of His weather
Fired gunshots, during His silent days to make the clouds rain
To prevent sneeze, to stink and spread
Complete with the heads of the fallen ghosts
And, adulterated saints
Stare from niches; nose blocked with antiseptic cotton-balls
Fingers counting piranhas in the ceramic fish-bowl
Or was it just the finger-bowl?

74

Ask at the Temple of Labyrinth
Why is that dog yellow? But was it not yellow?
The tail-less tale was the story we read at convent school
Eventually, the riddle of the Great Dog was solved
Swollen Feet became the King in the sardonic legend
He was left-handed to nullify his walking right
Not to specific; to the real time and real space
Jogeshwari among Goddess, became slum of hot-holes
Riots fueled Yellow Nation to animal-hood resort
Lost in perpetual maze, pleasant prayers are sounded
To the Labyrinth
Disciplined queue is formed to screw ritually, a whore-self
It was not an existential rape
It was an endowment exercise for a dead Dog

75

Her brittle body painted with a durable form
Pen and ink on paper
A desert varnish to paint married woman's womb
It indifferently houses the father of her son's unhinged love
Barricade to screen evil eye's protrusion
In between the Two eyes, it is the Third eye – blind
To banish exigencies, the Look is necessary to Gaze

76

The fast is to dry the stomach
It is Concocted Coercion Confronting the Cause
Pangs pull the petulant pants down; to discipline
A pertinent punishment is a subversive vocabulary
To dispassionately tame the obedient self

77

Flamboyant house of yours, in the collective commune; callow
Drainpipe outlets into you. Waste teeming, overspreads
Ghalib spouts couplets through the meandering mouth
In the bathroom
His urges of a thousand desires dies wet
"*Kafir*! You popped again in my life of love"

78

Vulgar brute falls into You to enlarge our feeble lineage
Causative queries and a pink penis-sheath is used
"Mother, will you get pregnant again?"
Oedipus, of the dichromatic comic strip, I had not read
Rheumatic Grandmother
Oblivious, shrug-pass an optimistic hump
Sleep, eat, sleep throughout the birth-point-time
Grim copulation, misfired in the right direction
My left-hand consort freely roams in an *ikat* wrap-around
To make it easy, without noise

79

Three on an Enfield, resurrected into a Harley Davidson
A nervous cycle on the *dickey* of an *Ambassador*
Ruggedly trotting
They don't meet, but multiple lives interchange
Vehicles are driven on a circuitous highway
Smooth without potholes
No unconditional accident occurs
And they pass by, smiling at each other's unbearable dexterity

80

"When was the son older than the father?"
In a triptych created, the Divine Kingdom talks in opposites
Three God-heads belligerently quarrel
Attached to One-head-ness
In the reversal of allocation, fickle truth changes colors
On an ordinary holiday
They sleep and the World is drawn in a void dream
We then, become devoted sons of our fastidious fathers
And not, savage father of our erratic sons

81

Bitter tears of myself, not from my moist eyes only
But from everyone's Third Eye
They who see the Me, shall cry furiously
Said He of the Me fame
Nicely murdered, where the three roads meet hesitatingly
Only one generous fly
A crippled cockroach
And, a clumsy spider keep watch
Before He died, he aspired to be an unknown Hexapod
And, mother in one womb, a hundred Tetrapods
But was sheepishly killed before any Motherhood

82

In the Inherent, functions are not constantly questioned
Answers are not given on essentiality
"Who am I? I am Who?"
The meanings of Things are known
Still. At bedtime

83

From a conceited quadrangle of curious queries
Crooked representations are envisaged
Contempt corroborated
Entrenched in the Earth Division of Life
Gracious ascent punctures into a free fall
Returns to the Sky Show Shadows of Life

84

An incandescent headgear; gargantuan
Foggiest belief written on the crown of the quick quest
Instituted by the size-ice-capsule-of-collapse
Dharavi Notebook of mine, now I write
Was a smash-hit at the belligerent book-office
It boomeranged without returning

85

Cruel efficacy of soft sand, to murmur with wind
"Castle-stone erode when breeze talks with sand"
A maple-wood rolling-pin
Becomes a symbol of unspeakable protest. In the
Kingdom of selfish children, sand castles are silently smashed
"Mother in enemy's garb or enemy in mother's garb?"
Rest will be known when I grow Big
To see. To hear. To talk. And. To do
Dowry she got, was my mother's only joy
In her Kingdom though, children carry sandbags
To a Catholic school

86

No sensible cat can stay in this City of Love
With soft hands we dip silver swords in tomato sauce
Ketchup, to substitute ghastly blood of goats
Street-Walking in theory
We end up in an eloquent whorehouse of submissive wives
Selling cane furniture and brittle red *bindis*
Those who are on Earth, fly-by-wire and crash
We who wallow in our wicked walks
Enter depressed whirlpools and frugal spirals
Hunted in whorls of the City's non-doing, we are forgotten, fast
Looking up in the dark sky of the night life
We saw only once: Ursa Major crisply falling into Ursa Minor

87

Once upon a gay, work-horn time, sleep overcomes
During the oath taking moment
The fragmentary orgasm is narrowly missed
Fidelity pursued in haste by tender foot, loses by inches
Candid confession jumbles in a Mediterranean dream
Titillating her cruel clitoris, his tongue-speechless; sour tasting
Two years gloss over a forgiven kiss with a toothbrush-pubic
It was an era of War and Bruises
Love was nimbly born again, deaf between withered bust-size

88

Haunted horticulturist's enigma
Of car by-lane flattened with flowers
In the city where he generously disembarked
Alike, to a tin tube light blinking seriously
Unable to withstand the efforts of daylight's intrusion
To let flowers grow we need the sun to come in
The farmer's dream in him, he left at the bed-corner
He affectionately walked over the flowers
And, sniffed the foul smell
The cantankerous cars were flying above
The fetid air, once again

89

To Bless, is like to Bow, is like to be No More
Shining, boot polished shoes or dusty sweet smelling feet?
Father's feet and Mother's land, ventured
Whenever I return to go again
Grow old in the sad beginning and still live long
Till the end; before The End
Slept through life but made to live longer
Ram said He wanted a Queen
And, not a Washer-man's figmentation
In fire we all die, even the Not-Blessed angels

90

Were you the fish-worker on a hunger strike?
On a podium cross-legged
Fish bone hung to desolate locks – staring blankly
Smile of a hunched man-in-skeleton, remembered, thoughtfully
Panasonic camcorder zooms on
To the decayed teeth plucking putrid flesh
Anand makes a film, slowly
He lacks comprehension to proceed to the Great Sea Route
Without fish, the night sky is not dark, only stars' smile
When the eye of the storm is blind
Why hunger is prone to protest?

91

Confluence of three rivers
The Unseen, the Seen, the Overseen
Three rivers meet: two dead, other dying. Sacred spot is
Renamed. Piquancy forbidden
Weight sinks to touch the sleek Python
Fire and Water Dreaming
Chanting the canticles of the Lord, the river is born
In the Self. *Saraswati* was discovered at last – sad
Under my tarpaulin umbrella, all the three rivers live

92

Where did you not venture, with your Dancing Mask?
Outstretched legs enter your senile space. Empty is the Future
In between the threshold, it fortunately forms a bold Future

93

The contrite sprit eschews
And, outbreaks as an authentic performance
Desire to volunteer is a miracle play – abridged
Ceremony is received here; from the sensuous woman of Spire
The circumcision bloodied at the Dog Mountain; fast
In the Machine-time time, Dream stops and
Sleep overcomes. Heard is the sound between two islands
Earth was created
When a head of little Kangaroo and body of armored Snake
Circled Sand as it slipped mutely

94

Satire through idiosyncrasies of sad conjectures
Known conventionally through dots of passage
A pretentious mode, caught
Read, re-read a sacred site's diabolical dialogues
The tendency to except residence on land is classical
But the night sky still belongs to a tactile surface

95

Balloon driver flying above the alabaster cathedral
Snaps at the white ants below
On the one-way road towards the wind-ward eye
In the line with Frigate Bird, meandering straight
Warm air escapes through leather jackets covering; feather soft
Devil bone in the bone bundle migrate to a waterhole
Made by the desolate woman
In me, they make me up, these bones
For the first time torn away from the earth, a wayward assault
The voyage with my father remains Untitled
At the power-site, I am buried with my unforsaken bones
Where was it, the death of a Father's son is flown hot?

96

A Pop Art motif
Effervescence, pageantry and cloistered revelry
The artiste with popcorn created it. Seen from behind
On a tee-shirt it is a Question & Answer formality
A gaze penetrating the Yoni of a Yantra of Art
The colorful tree that *Raza* made, uproots a heritage protected
A ribbed condom was used to omit laxity
When the Art did not pop-up
A neglected ceremony to bury it in repetition
Assured its vicious end
In mass production

97

The Whorehouse Syndrome struck vivaciously
Rescued from a Screw
Nuts and Bolts continue to feverishly fuck
Men in Modern Times forget Chaplin, fast. Very fast
Only the Heroine remembers, behind a barbed wire
Her Hero, only smiled, like Raj Kapoor

98

In the English speaking tradition, box-office hit
Is a movie, moving with the temple of Labyrinth
And people washing their souls, huddled together
Watch Yeah! See Yeah! Cry Yeah!

99

Grim reaper of an imaginative re-enactment
Created the Alps in the Book of Shadows
When the inner order of adepts thought simultaneously
Red roses and the Golden crosscut saw the initiated disappear
Of love, sex and Holy Ghost
Xeroxing each other's conditioning
On a plastic Canon machine

100

Forbidden promises and funky town follies, forever forgiven
I saw ten of them – Mangal Pandey and his Sepoy Mutiny
In the Condom-Galli
Shouting in the memories of affectionate Trees
Sedate slogans to protect a hundred and forty-year-old image
A war fought; commenced with mutineers in Sadhu's garb
Distributing *chapattis*
At Aligarh, Etawah, Gorakhpur and Lucknow
Free; to all who vowed not to use guns and cartridges
That reeked of cows and pigs
A pious war lost; torn in shreds by cannon-fire
And confined till death in Rangoon
Latter hung from naked Trees, who remembered

101

Covering the consequences of innocence
A fastidious sobriety; virulent
Infuriated by acrimonious poachers, playing truant
Akka, alludes the monthly ill of the feminine sex
The Holy of Holies can be passed through the bloody door
Nuances of a flying reindeer flashes on the screen
Skeptical acquiescence concedes an unfinished defeat
Curiously, the inquisitive apathy remains swollen
And a reticent muse, cleverly hoodwinks a revered expert

102

Furious fuzziness, frowns at the fast flowing mouse
Free in old washing machine and a new Pentium 586
It is in the habit of penetrating
The heretic of modern time ducks a man centered Inquisition
Passing judgement at the female pronoun, frequently
It reluctantly joins those who hide above the sun
Punching pink, plastic buttons
Staring blinking, blind tube-lights
A turquoise thunderbird clan with gun-stock war-club
Frantically joins them in search
All over the overburdened cosmos
For a body as sinful, lustful and violent
As the good old Devil, with a silver lap-top

103

The radio-factory crying; in need of a brittle soliloquist
To retain the good taste as an aftermath
A point-blank answer in common parlance
To utter faithfully, is to deliver without mouthing a fetid talk

104

North is the conquest in the side of the power
Reckless in need to masquerade
The naked heel of the hero
Does not touch the variegated earth
But its direction is constant in every compass
Converging, at the end of the point lotus-feet
Brutalized by nature it assumes its devastating Form
It is the door; here the Gods were born
Formed by numbness of a furtive fossilized fortune

105

Corroded fate is the flower-girdle around the headless neck
Original equation unsubstantiated by its figure. When
In-house, a pot full of rye swallow corrective stanzas
An afternoon, full of monsoon, acknowledges
Self-hood-ness. Flowers bloom in flooded street corner
At an instance, turning to see, of self, is consolidated
Through a picturesque past, the holiday fever catches on
The neck approaches death in a conclusive fashion
The flower vase is empty once again

106

Were there hogs at the bottom of the Hogg Street?
They ran amok when the new market burnt
My mother saw them, not in her dreams but LIVE
A caught-in-the-sinking-reminiscence phenomenon
I saw the mourning, at the death of no one – but bones
Of toy horse and plastic cycles, I rode on
As a child lost in the maze. The center had
A World War one cannon aimed at nonchalance
In the fire, it melted stoically

107

A silver spoon tossed in a newborn's sink
To twist the spinal-cord or make its tongue salty
The death was not withstanding a defeat
I was a father bewildered at the sight of the hedgehog
How could she deliver a baby in a carton of a television?
Pages of a telephone directory smeared with blood, wrapped
A straight umbilical cord, dry as a bone
The grotesque was a happy site to roll a camera on
Death was in the other frame, just coming. Please wait
In the darkened room you sat on chairs
To see me dying without death in the pine-flower chamber

108

The warranted action of demise is essential
At the end of the crooked tail ending story
The ethical, solemnly footloose, during moral ambivalence
And liberation through supermarket imperialism
Is accessed. Metallic smelling
That was during the twilight of duty-hour
Nothing is obligatory; only buying means being

109

Gods lined neatly in rows gasp at resoluteness
Of lame man selling them, and
The female mother haggling
Of stone, the erect phallus wonders why?
In the street of Days, No-one is an obligation
And nothing is a problem
The heavenly melodrama of Ages is televised
Again and Again
Within the melodramatic space of the idiot box. Universe
Is understood as seen through the satellite
Channels intermingle and television is the new God
Made in stone they are not forgotten

110

In the absence of a dexterous grandfather, a family threatens
To buy home-space in the memory of the Original
A nuclear family or an unclear wisdom?
The son can also die before the father
Like in *Shakti*
Amitabh Bachchan and Dilip Kumar floated in mid-air
Of an airport seen by train to the Start
The assumption of life tortures the weakened shoulders
Love could not stay, but lived in the grandchild
The cancer rotted and the man lived to see its death
After fourteen days' ancestors were beckoned
Like every year, at dawn, the three rivers meet simultaneously

111

At the God centered Last Supper
The only son, was betrayed by his left hand
His own celestial body was the closeted work
Of the divine devil
In the cloistered congregation, the better half transformed
Into the icon of the Church's apparent weapon
The wordless aphorisms with deliberate ideology
Widely celebrated
Spreads into the beholder's munificent world
To harshly grasp, is to examine the true realization of
The dense display
And adapt to the art of baroque Veneration

112

Absolute terrorized death is known as divine devastation
Sacrifice the living; and the headless mother is pleased
The widowed virgin needs blood-faith
She is misunderstood, for the perpetual pregnancy
Is *Yama's* curse to his own wife, turned potent?
Vulgar taboo is again sought to enrich compassion
Life-Lords in the run-of-the-mill gesticulations
The violence in coming together
Of the two incommensurable principles
Leads to life dying and giving birth to life
Without any anticipatory nostalgia. Death and Life

113

If it rains in your mournful dream
Then it is an incurable problem
The space full of sentimental faces gets wet; colors fade
You will not recognize them split
Over each other. "Sujata, why do I comc in your dreams"?
Through thought, you also loose the maroon umbrella

114

In the memory of the naked tree, the wide-bottom space
Is created, like bell-bottom concealing
The legs of sixties on block heels
The indulgent man, yesterday was found hiding. He who
Saw the earth-seed sprout into a hiding space
In the hide-and-seek of life, my precocious wife always won
"I spy, one two, three. You are out"
The sacred space is dangerously empty
Today through its haziness
I spy, Sujata away from me

115

What's the weight of a dead man falling ponderously?
The subtle change in gesture between the ends in a space
Is the same. Look into them
The fall does not end. The land moves below it
For an answer, even the reason to knock
An empty door is valid. The door-less room is full
Of empty space. The finite man continues to fall, vapidly

116

In the theological space
Distraught Gods are consecrated conscientiously
Daubed with mother color; agility is cautiously withdrawn
Money was invested in the benediction of content
The hybrid aesthetics were bought
To be sold in the market place of questions
Nauseating images of his own-self, hammered at the town hall
She bought it, who reincarnated to be his only wife
The twenty-seventh *Avatar* was jailed last week, for polygamy
There he met the holy scamster, who duped him
Aside: "The earlier Godfathers were actually genuine"

117

Through the broken vestibule beyond open space
Agile among the triviality, a bronze firmament
Nataraj performing the spectacle of worldly creations
Every moment, each atom is a masterpiece destroyed
Abandoning my astral body on the fourth navel of awareness
The lump of time, that I saw, is an apparatus empty
Consigned to the fire between day and night.
Every day. Every Night

118

Fallen in the eyes of darkness, angel overhauls
Opens the metal knob of a pale window
To see a red horse passing
Takes a random shot; leaps into the forbidden experiment
In love, God was the Devil and Devil was the God
At the vexed position you will see him praying patiently
Your Father thou art in Hell
Holy be your Fame
Here is the ordinary angel, is tempting your soul
Actually both God and Devil, are one
Two fast friends
One debilitating system of retrieval
But many forsaken followers

119

Only in the wild city the Suburbia was born
Hung till death, in suspension, between the metropolis
And the hamlet. Life, lives a civic emancipation
After death
Automatic subversion seizes the opportunity to strike
It allows man to commute from end-to-end
The further he transcends, the closer he lives in it
There is that fluctuation, snapping the ends
In Suburbia, we herd for God's sake

120

Fondling an overused arse
The whore house joint, enjoys a weather-beaten image
A rough hand caresses a full-blown balloon
To screw it from behind is to bust a buddy's bright bosom
The fart-smell travels far and wide

121

The perfect pause in the drop, is sternly prohibited
Using distorted looks of imagination. Reality
Is irreducible reeled into
The sacred end, in the void duration
The perfect pause in the drop, is sternly prohibited
Because during real-time, distortion is virtually impossible

122

The gallant types are often crucified
On the iron cross, at the cross-road of a cross section
Cosmetic application by the lady of the blue night
Adds red to her dry lips
Languorously, through the wide open birth-shaft
The passage-wager, induces a false born to pop
The Shaman of the Stars was the professional mid-wife to a
Sprout, pronounced and natural
"Will this type survive the tenth time?"

123

To be shot, while protesting is a severe end
.303 is the magical wand that transforms us
"Weight-less life momentarily experiences weight-fullness"

124

Silky, green blouse, and maroon sticking to the cracked lips
False bosom of stuffed hankies; doused with *itar*
Balanced on plastic stilettos and see through shapes
The dusky face walks with its mutilated self
A man's leg, a blue panty, and a dangling *mangalsutra*
Chee! When all is threatened to be exposed

125

Shattered ear drums; the dead dream woke me up
El-Nino warm waters does not pause
The melancholic monsoon falls endlessly on weekends. Wet
Spoilt days also end at night. Dry
We reinforce concrete dreams with our own sincere eyes. Shut
At the collapse of the Day-Dreamer's dense desire
The weary world was born on the seventh day; all alone

126

To ceaselessly travel in a direction-less direction
Is to end at the dead end with the dead
At the other side, the new city begins folding its own lust
At this side, my new city ends without love
Trapped, I go to a convent school in a cramped school-bus
To keep in touch with unfinished
Home-work and menacing Class-work

127

A formidable spirit announces a mind boggling Seek
The revolutionary idea was to uproot
Gods in malfunctioning History
Malevolent stones abound by a mechanical structure is a curse
A Holy Place is desecrated
The foolish intentions sparked a precarious prohibition
Sujata, please forgive me, for you are my polite Goddess
It really was like going from the other side
Of the surrounding worldview
Into the circumambulatory void
Of congealed causation

128

A perfunctory approach is always superficial
Unrelentingly scratching the dreary surface
The nails only get sharpened
Blood-red becomes hot-pink; pale-blue becomes sky-blue
Bottle-green becomes grass-green; with scratches
To deal with any formidable issue, dry depth is essential
Down you go, till you drown
Nails were always cell-less entities without life
They survive the deep approach

129

Dark-blue forest; cool!
Tyranny sobers an intoxicated brute
Swarthiness of the flesh color soothes the eyes
Shave the land of its cover; heedlessly
An unfeigned candor speaks the perfect truth
This is just a forlorn forest, full of wild trees and green animals

130

Millions of heads composing the song of Songs
At the Break, Two was ahead of One
Hindi is the tongue of the whole country; flapping turgidly
A sad literature of a poet-turned-lyricist
Garland of songs reap prizes in a sitcom
On the stage; in the limelight; before an audience
At the dining table we are the inanimate creatures
Imitating *Lata Mangeshkar*
Staring an Idiot

131

Low valley of comfort and virgin possibilities. Pregnant
Crawling to grow Big. Submissive to vocalization
Mute spectator to the Life, breathing; alive
Assault has to be prevented
Before men wage wars to kill themselves, in unison
In the evening of the ever-green heroism
Amitabh dies in the valley of his career-graph

132

Tabalchi; hurtling from *ek-taal* to *teen-taal*, never stops
Shuttling between two sound-full space; cohesively coaxed
Captive of a chunk of beats, called up by Him
Heaven's womb were terrible twins in tandem
Like Laurel & Hardy thumbed vigorously
From the quintessential quiet
Emerged deaf God's own elliptical rhythm

133

The bathtub aquarium is a colorful enterprise
Overflowing, we swim in search to wreck our lively lives
Catfish collage is seen from the frozen hermit's peerless gaze
The enlightening stage of the cross-bone construction
Only the skull-bowl was missing when we play pirates

134

Shradh in the family, is the excuse
Not to meet
Why feed the flying dead, when ancestors live with us?
Unacquainted still alive; fallen, still pulsating
My mother would feed her father-in-law, everyday
Before dawn
The albino crow would wake the whole sleeping family
My father was happy to see his father, eating
Till death occurred once again

135

When the question of authenticity arises
The mechanical master who teaches, disappears
During actual transformation
At the tender threshold, his need was essential
But now he is the dark door. When
To knock and to pass and to enter and to go
Is to be known and told
He guided me, in each of my preemptive life

136

In death, a question pregnant with me, answered
In a jiffy
Vitriolic thought about no-more, I see it through
The gaping mouth. *Vac* – unsounded, unheard, unknowable
But deafens my ears. Through it I still hear
Reused utility of colored water Tonics – fatal
Sealed in the backyard of a toilet-cleaner's life
Billu sold its grace to me. And I did not die desolately
But *Rajdhani* made him shiver sonorously, my maternal *mama*
Before his dying death

137

In the course of the day, the sun sets
In the west
At night, the fake eyes roll on
And, finally the whole thing collapses; but slowly

138

Willingness to work
Is to be admonished to feel vague
Because of the right-handed flicker
Of the tube-light. Was I, who switched
It on? Behind the Golden Dawn
The diamond fireflies lose their essence to fly forever
And light was all
That I saw

139

Cross-roads of the Sea
At the Sea-Saw Point in my futile garden
Of a fake dream that comes true
We don't use plastic nail-cutters
Just taciturn tongue, soft teeth and stony touch
The torrid taste that waters my polished mouth
Is in you. Salty. Sujata

140

Crucified Santa Claus is my fatigued Spirit
The commercial God in the era of bygone sales-man-ship
They sold me an electronic watch without numbers
That was found in an underwear
At Christmas Eve; folly followed by a fool
A meaningless triad
All resurrected with an Epilogue

141

Vociferous instinct is a cure to be fulfilled
In the thirsty land of the Heaven's Fate
"Were you forgotten? Was I lost?"
After a very long time, I write to you
A soft prayer at the edge of my florid destiny
That will be fulfilled
When I am nurtured by my juvenile mother
Before my death, I was alive
Before I lived, I was dead

142

That which pervades and meditates softly
Is a molten ice-cream
To make love to her
Honesty betrays the very essence of the pen
The red ink in it, spills an erotic love letter
Finally finished; I ended an alliterative verse

143

"We shall be poets once again"
Or was it only me who wants to pen myself, again?
After an unbelievable gap, to solicit images, grotesque
On tender texture which is called paper
Fearing doubt, a creative upsurge is let wantonly loose
Lost again in its wretched infancy
The promiscuous poet wonders his ponderous defeat

144

A greedy voyeurist commits a *faux pas*
He withheld other's anguished dreams
While they commit a mistake
To see from behind a wired-zone
His blue *burkha* slides to the wrong side
While ladies compartment gives apart, in fury

145

Fed up with me in the later years of her emboldened life
My servile mother serves me boiled vegetables and wheat-grass
She sees pinholes as big-holes in her silk saree of yore
God belittles her expectation to live
In my undying dreams, she is also my perplexed wife-to-be

ASHISH AVIKUNTHAK is a filmmaker whose films have been shown worldwide in film festivals, galleries, and museums. He has a PhD for Stanford University and now teaches at the University of Rhode Island. *Totem Spirit* is his first book of poems, published twenty years after they were written.